A Redneck's Guide to Financial Freedom

Sure-Fire Ways to Git Outta Debt and Accumulate Wealth!

A Redneck's Guide to Financial Freedom

Sure-Fire Ways to Git Outta Debt and Accumulate Wealth!

Richard W. Headrick

Hellfighter Publications

Published by Hellfighter Publications
One Freedom Square, Laurel, MS 39440-3367

ISBN 978-0-9787573-7-3

Library of Congress Control Number: 2008933192

First Printing 20,000 copies (January 1999)
Second Printing 20,000 copies (2001)
Third Printing 20,000 copies (2003)
Previously released as How to Escape Financial Bondage

Cover art and illustrations by Terry "Buzz" Busbea

Appreciation

Terry Busbea has been my friend since 1972. That was the year he joined our company and became our art director. He has faithfully performed his duties and created many well-known symbols used today in industry and commerce worldwide.

His willingness to help me and Gina "look good" in projects such as this one is "over the top."

Buzz, as he is affectionately known by those of us who love him, designed the cover and drew all the illustrations herein. He is the bestest of the best and we know you'll agree as you see his creative ability displayed throughout these pages.

Dedication

Wayne and Jan Nichols, aka Big Daddy and Little Mama, are two of the "goodest" rednecks I know. All their lives they have cared for others.

They always buy things on sale and then take the savings and spend it on those in need. They also have a gift to "sniff out" good deals and, having learned how to use SELF-DISCIPLINE, they are debt free.

They have everything they need and most of what they want. How do they do it? They work hard, budget properly, spend wisely and aren't extravagant.

Big Daddy and Little Mama are the perfect example of a family that truly has financial freedom. It is for this, and many other reasons, that Gina and I dedicate this book to them.

Contents

Introduction

Many moons ago, a friend and I started a little business to help folks less fortunate than us obtain small loans for emergency needs.

Over the course of several years we saw that some of our customers used their loan proceeds to buy things they didn't need. We saw them use their borrowings for self-indulgences. We saw them use their borrowed money to participate in games of chance. We watched them waste it on many non-beneficial things.

Deciding to do something that might help each of them learn SELF-DISCIPLINE, rebuild their character and station in life, and take better care of their money, I wrote this book.

We are no longer in the small loan business, but what I saw and learned during those years showed me what it was like to be bound by debt. Debt is a demon that will destroy you, your family, and your business, if you don't know how to handle it.

I earnestly desire that you, and anyone else who puts into practice what I have written, will escape financial bondage, obtain financial freedom and accumulate more money than you've ever had in your life.

CHAPTER 1

How'd You Git in this Mess in the First Place?

Your current job doesn't pay enough? Lost the job you had? Ran out of money? Got too much debt? Drugs got a hold on you? Can't say no to the bottle? Divorced? She got the goldmine and you got the shaft?

Tried your luck at the casinos and found out the only luck you had was bad? Can't make ends meet, regardless of what you do? If your answer is "yes" to any of these questions, then keep on reading and you may find the solution to your problem.

Many of us, at one time or another, have been right where you may be now; broke or close to it and seemingly flat out of luck. Some people, however, will allow themselves to wallow around in this condition for the rest of their lives, but others will get out of their financial dilemma by overcoming the obstacles that got them there in the first place.

To help you focus on your objective, I want you to memorize this old saying:

Two men looked through prison bars,
One saw mud, the other stars.

What this little proverb means is, one of the prisoners in this particular jail is still feeling sorry for himself and has his head hanging real low; therefore, his eyes only see the muddy mire of despair he has gotten himself into.

It's true, when we're feeling low we seem to look down not up. This guy has not yet realized, that he and he alone is responsible for his being in jail. He committed a crime and now he's paying the price for his lack of SELF-DISCIPLINE in his life.

The other inmate, the one looking up and seeing the stars, has already realized he's made a mistake, but he's not looking down wallowing in his misery. No, siree, he's looking up and thinking of what he's gonna do with the rest of his life when he gets out of jail. He knows he never wants to be in bondage again.

Life is sometimes like a jail, isn't it? In my opinion it is, so let's compare the two and see if you might agree. *IN JAIL*, some prisoners are on death row, some are in solitary confinement, some are in regular cells and some are soon to be parolees who will regain the freedoms prisoners don't have. *IN LIFE*, some folks live on "death row" because they've given up trying to succeed. They have resigned themselves to live on the death row of defeat the rest of their lives.

Some folks are in "solitary confinement" because they don't have the courage to "break free" and do what it takes to get ahead. They continue to do stupid things because they lack SELF-DISCIPLINE and remain in their solitary confinement of poor judgment.

Some are prisoners of habits. Each habit has them locked in a "cell" of bondage and until they break these habits, they can never enjoy the freedom to succeed. The rest of us are parolees. We've made mistakes and errors in judgment, but we've overcome them and can now walk around freely enjoying some of the niceties of life. But, if we don't use SELF-DISCIPLINE, we are all apt to mess up again.

Remember, life is *sometimes* like a jail. Not all the time mind you, just when we let it imprison us. When we're broke and without money, when we're at odds with our family members or when we're spiritually defeated, we land back in the "jail of life" and are deprived of the things we want and enjoy.

This little book will hopefully help you get off the death row of financial imprisonment. We hope it will help you get out of solitary confinement by helping you gain the courage and SELF-DISCIPLINE you need to make something of yourself. Hopefully it will help you bust open your prison cell of financial bondage and show you how to experience the freedom of a parolee as you make your way up the ladder of prosperity that will, in time, set you TOTALLY FREE from financial difficulties and help you achieve financial freedom and accumulate for yourself a stash of cash.

REDNECK PROVERB #1:
THE SECRET TO SUCCESS IS
SWEAT, CALLOUSES & COMMONSENSE!

CHAPTER 2

What're You Doin' Right Now to Succeed Financially?

I know you're probably working hard, but are you working hard enough?

Are you working 8 hours a day or 16 hours a day?

Are you too lazy to work? Are you living off Uncle Sam? Or maybe even your in-laws?

Do you "hang one on" every Friday or Saturday night?

Are your eyes all glazed over from the joint or fix you had last night?

Is your girlfriend draining you of all you've got and ruining your marriage, too?

Is alimony and child support eating you up?

How are your lungs? Can't breathe because of too many cigarettes?

Did you gamble last week's paycheck away?

Are you living above your means?

None of the above, but still can't make ends meet? Maybe it's because you don't have a plan.

Businesses, families, and individuals need to have a budget to operate efficiently. If you don't have one, then the time has come for you to come up with one and see exactly where you are financially.

> IF YOU DON'T KNOW WHERE YOU ARE, CHANCES ARE, YOU'LL NEVER GET TO WHERE YOU'RE GOING!

Let's begin with a simple overview of your financial position right now. On the next page, fill in the blanks with the amount you spend each month on each line item.

OVERVIEW SHEET

INCOME:	MONTHLY
INCOME from your job	$
Extra INCOME from odd jobs	$
Extra INCOME from government subsidies	$
Extra INCOME from child support or alimony	$
Other INCOME	$
TOTAL MONTHLY INCOME:	**$**
EXPENSES:	
Alcohol and Beer	$
Alimony	$
Car Payment	$
Child Support	$
Cigarettes	$
Clothes	$
Credit Card Debt (total monthly payments)	$
Daycare	$
Drugs – legal	$
Drugs – illegal	$
Electricity	$
Entertainment	$
Fast Food/Restaurants	$
Gas Bill	$
Gasoline/Diesel	$
Groceries	$
House Insurance	$
House Maintenance	$
House Payment or Rent	$
Internet	$
Loan Payment to:	$
Loan Payment to:	$
Loan Payment to:	$
Maintenance on Vehicles	$
Medical Bills	$
Miscellaneous Monthly Expenses:	$
Miscellaneous Monthly Expenses:	$
Miscellaneous Monthly Expenses:	$
Phone/Cell Phone Bill	$
School (books, tuition, etc.)	$
Tithe to your church (10% of total income)	$
Truck Payment	$
TV Cable	$
Water Bill	$
TOTAL MONTHLY EXPENSES:	**$**

SUMMARY

TOTAL MONTHLY INCOME		$
TOTAL MONTHLY EXPENSES	minus (-)	$
WHAT'S LEFT **(or how much you're short!)**	**equals (=)**	**$**

Now that you understand how much you owe and how little money you have left after you pay your obligations, how do you feel? Pretty bad, huh? Read on anyway, **hope** is coming!

Is your outgo more than your income? If so, you've got a problem. But don't panic or fall into a pit of despair. THERE IS HOPE! *("For I know the plans that I have for you," declares the* L*ORD, "plans for welfare and not for calamity*

(financial hardships) *to give you a future and a hope."* Jeremiah 29:11, NASB)

The answers necessary to get you out of this mess may not be pleasant for you to hear or do, but if you'll buckle down and use SELF-DISCIPLINE, better times will lie ahead for you.

Read, with careful attention, the following chapters and see if they won't lend some insight as to how you can do something positive toward improving your financial condition.

CHAPTER 3

Stop the Bleedin'

In 1990, I almost lost everything, and I was one sad puppy. I had worked all my life to get ahead and in 1989, I considered myself a success. I had a nice house, a fine truck, an airplane, a good business, with many men working for me, and I was making a lot of money.

Disaster, however, came swiftly. In 1990, nobody wanted to buy my product anymore so, sales fell to nothing almost overnight. I owed every bank in town and when I couldn't repay them, they started to foreclose on me. I saw myself losing everything that I had worked all my life to achieve. **I WAS NOW A PRISONER OF MY OWN STUPIDITY FOR BORROWING MORE MONEY THAN I COULD EVER PAY BACK!**

> HE WHO BORROWS SELLS HIS FREEDOM

However, I DID NOT WALLOW IN MY PITY nor did I hang my head down and look at the muddy mire of despair. No, siree, I looked up, saw the stars, and got me a plan together. Then I went to each of my creditors and explained to them that I had been a fool. I told them that I had obligated myself for more debt than I could handle, but if they would give me time, I'd pay them every penny I owed them.

All but one bank agreed to let me make smaller monthly payments. Some of the banks gave me a few months in which I didn't have to pay them anything. Some of my suppliers even let me pay them fifty cents on the dollar.

Let me explain what fifty cents on the dollar means. I owed one company $1,000 for some metal parts. I called the owner and told him that

I couldn't pay him the $1,000 I owed him and on top of that, it looked like I might be going broke. I asked him if he could cut me a little slack and discount my debt. If he would, I'd try to pay him immediately. I told this supplier that I had $500 and if he would take it as payment in full, I'd send it to him that day. He graciously accepted and I saved $500, or fifty cents on the dollar.

You may owe some debts you can't pay that have been a burden to you for a long time. If so, we've got work to do!

First, call your creditors and ask them to give you a discount. Tell them that you'll pay them in full "right now" if they will. Ask them if they will take fifty cents on the dollar. Most creditors who haven't received any money from you in a long time will jump at the chance to get "something." If you succeed, you will relieve a burden off your mind, a debt off your budget's balance sheet and your creditor will get a little of his money back, too.

One thing to remember, if you owe someone who doesn't think you'll ever pay, he may take as little as twenty-five cents on the dollar. Which means, if you owe a guy $100 he might take $25 to settle the debt. I know it can be done because I did it several times when I was almost broke. Chances are, you've got credit card debt too. If so, call your credit card company and offer them the same deal, I betcha they will take it! Don't read this and say, “Richard is full of bull, nobody’s gonna take twenty-five cents for a dollar of debt.” **I KNOW THEY WILL BECAUSE THEY DID IT FOR ME!** Not everybody will and not everybody can, but some creditors will. If you call them and they say no, then call ’em again next month because their collection policies may change or maybe you'll get to talk to a different collection person who will be more understanding.

The point is, DON'T GIVE UP! Keep on

keeping on! Keep hammering away for discounts!

If you do get your creditors to give you a discount on your debt, be sure to remember them when you achieve financial freedom. If they give you fifty cents off each dollar of your debt to help you out, then give the balance back to them when you can afford to do so. It's the right thing to do. It's called working together.

The second thing to do is this, if you owe too much money for something that you can't pay for and you can't get the creditor to take a discount on the payments, then sell the bloody thing that's causing you to be in financial bondage.

When I almost went broke, I sold everything that was costing me a nickel to keep.

I had two vehicles; I kept my truck and sold my car. I had two phone lines coming into my apartment; I disconnected one of them. I had a boat and I sold it. I had an airplane and I sold it. I had a nice piece of property that I thought I would one day build a house on; I sold it too. I sold everything that I did not have to have. I even quit going to the barbershop and started cutting my own hair!

I did whatever it took to lower my expenses to the bare minimum and I encourage you to do the same. If you don't have anything to sell, try the following measures.

If you're smoking two packs of cigarettes a day, cut back to one pack a day (or better yet, cut out smoking all together). This one move alone will save you $4.00 per day or $120 per month. Imagine saving enough money to pay your electric bill or at least buy one school lunch per day (at $2.00 each) for one of your kids, and still have $76 left over to pay on some other bill you owe.

If something costs a nickel to own, get rid of it. If you're driving a big old, gas-guzzling

Cadillac just so you'll look good, SELL IT! We're not talking *looks* here. We're talking financial commonsense. So, get rid of the Caddy and buy a small, fuel-efficient, compact car or truck. You may not look as cool, but you'll be saving big bucks that can then be used to pay down other debts.

If you're buying high-priced clothes at high price stores just for the label, STOP! Go to a Hudson Salvage Center, or a similar type store, that sells slightly damaged and closeout merchandise at a fraction of the cost. Chances are, you'll find the same labels and styles that you would normally find in many high price stores.

Don't let your pride keep you in financial bondage. LEARN TO BE THRIFTY!

My wife and I have a wardrobe full of Hudson's clothes, shoes, accessories, and jewelry. I even found a great pair of sunglasses there for eighty-eight cents and have never had so many compliments on a pair of sunglasses in my life. The deals are plentiful at Hudson's and if they don't have what you *need* in stock one day, go back a week later and they will probably have it in stock then.

Like I said earlier, if you don't know where you're going, it's pretty hard to get there. Well, the same thing is true of financial freedom. If you don't know how to get out of debt, then financial freedom may be a long way off. This means you've got to have a plan, a plan that will work for you!

If you filled out the Overview Sheet on page 9, you're either happy or sad. You either have enough income to pay your bills or you don't. If you do, good for you! If you don't, let's get to work!

First, we have to list the essentials for living. You have to have them unless you want to live on the street the rest of your life. So, let's get a plan together for obtaining the basics for life.

Following is an example of the basic monthly financial needs for a family of four:

	Proposed	Actual
House Payment or Rent	$ 400	$_____
Electricity, Water, Gas	175	_____
Car payment, Gasoline, Tag	400	_____
Food	400	_____
Clothes	100	_____
Medicine	150	_____
Miscellaneous	100	_____
	$1,725	$_____

In other words, an average family of four needs at least $1,725 per month "take home" money just to survive. Anything in addition to the basic items above can be done without. Oh, you may want the *niceties* of life, but you must first make sure the *necessities* of life are secured.

I wish there was a magic formula that would allow you to have everything you want, but I'm sad to say there's not. Most of the time, however, HARD WORK and SELF-DISCIPLINE will get you everything you *need* and most of what you *want*. But, you can't spend more than you take in without getting in trouble.

To get out of debt, the first thing you must do is STOP SPENDING! It doesn't make any difference how much or how little you spend; if it's more than you take in, you'll still go broke.

I entitled this chapter "Stop the Bleedin'." That simply means, **STOP YER OUTGO, BY STOPPIN' YER SPENDIN'!** Cut your cost of living any way you can. You know more about your situation than I'll ever know so you'll have to evaluate your ***needs*** from your ***desires*** and spend accordingly.

REDNECK PROVERB #3:

IF'N SOMETHIN' THAT YOU DON'T NEED COSTS YOU A NICKEL TO KEEP, GIT RID OF IT!

CHAPTER 4

Don't Obligate Yerself Fer More Than You Can Afford

Three friends and I were traveling along I-40 in Arkansas some time ago and in a heavy rainstorm we saw a stranded motorist. We stopped to help and found the motorist to be a young college student who couldn't afford a wrecker and whose father wouldn't come to help her. We helped her get going again and during the hour we were with her she made this statement, "Never want for something you can't have, then you can have everything you want."

Later, I thought to myself how profound that statement was and how uncomplicated life would be if we would keep our needs and desires simple and not let them become so extravagant that we have to sacrifice to have them.

Her words, "NEVER WANT FOR SOMETHING YOU CAN'T HAVE, THEN YOU CAN HAVE EVERYTHING YOU WANT" should be the watchword to financial planning.

- Some folks should never buy a tuxedo.
- Some folks should never buy a limousine.
- Some folks should never buy a jet airplane.
- Some folks should never buy a fancy house.
- Some folks should never buy a yacht.
- Some folks should never buy a vacation home.
- Some folks should never buy a Caribbean resort.

Why? Unless you can afford 'em, you can get by without 'em! But, of course, these are no-brainers. Who really *needs* any of that stuff anyway? Now, take a look at these things and see if they're a temptation, or maybe even a reality, for you:

- Some folks should never buy a brand new bass boat.
- Some folks should never buy the biggest four-wheeler on the market.
- Some folks should never buy mud tires for their pickup truck.
- Some folks should never buy an iPhone.
- Some folks should never buy season tickets to the NASCAR races.

Why? For the very same reason. Unless you can afford 'em, **you can get by without 'em!**

Our life's desire to gain material possessions is similar to our having lunch in a cafeteria. We see all this good stuff to eat and each item looks more delicious as we go down the line. We start putting everything we see on our plate and before we know it, our plate is full, our tray is full and our pocketbook is empty. Why? Because we bought more than we needed.

We all want nice things and there's nothing wrong with wanting nice things. However, most of us figure out ways to buy many of the things we *want*, but really don't *need*. We decide we want them, we think we have to have them and, come hell or high water, we're going to get them. Yep, we get them alright, but my, oh my, what a burden our selfish desires and undisciplined actions place on our finances!

Most of us know when we're gonna get our tax refund check. Right? Right! Have you already borrowed against it? Have you already spent it? I'm sad to say it, but most folks have.

As Americans, we are the most undisciplined people in the world. A Vietnamese or Filipino family will save, skimp, and do without many personal desires just to be able to come to America. When they get here, they will live like rats in some shack no bigger than your garage and spend only what is necessary to survive. I said, "to *survive*" not "to fulfill their *desires*"!

A family like that will work hard - sixteen to eighteen hours a day, six or seven days a week. They will live in near destitution for years until they have socked away a "nest egg" that will see them through troubled times. It's then, and only then, that they buy or build a small modest house. It's then, and only then, that they buy a reasonably priced vehicle, one that's perfectly suited for their needs.

We could learn a lesson of SELF-DISCIPLINE and PERSONAL DENIAL from these hard working people.

REDNECK PROVERB #4:
YOU CAN HAVE ANYTHANG YOU WANT,
IF'N...YOU DON'T SPEND
MOR' THAN YOU GOT!

CHAPTER 5

Habitz

We all have habits and many of them are hard to break. But, if you ever want to achieve financial freedom, you must break your bad habits.

ALCOHOL

When some folks are feeling low, they turn to strong drink.

You may say, "Hey, it's my business if I drink." Well, I hate to tell you this, my friend, but if you're married, and have children, it's not just your business, it's your family's business. If you're employed, it's not just your business, it's your employer's business. If you owe money, it's not just your business, it's your creditor's business.

You may say, "Hey, my bottle of whiskey only costs $10 and I can afford it! I've had a hard week at work and I need my space! This is my enjoyment, this is my pleasure!"

You say you can afford it. Well, let's look and see if you can really afford to drink a $10 bottle of whiskey every weekend.

First, if you drink a $10 bottle of whiskey each week, that's $520 per year. For most moderately sized homes, that's the electric or gas bill. It's enough to pay your phone bill. It could be used to pay for some of the fuel you use in your car. This $520 a year should be used to help reduce your debt thus increasing your wealth.

Second, if you drink that $10 bottle of whiskey on Friday night with the boys, you're going to deprive your wife and kids of having their husband/daddy at home with them for some good wholesome fellowship.

Third, if you drink that $10 bottle of whiskey on Saturday night, you definitely won't be in shape to go, as a family, to church on Sunday.

(I'm using the male gender in illustrations, but this same advice applies to the woman of the house too.)

Perhaps both of you, husband and wife, drink a $10 bottle of whiskey over the weekend. That's $1,040 per year wasted!

Your argument to that may be, “Hey, I don’t partake of the strong stuff!” Well, that’s great! But what about the 6-pack you drink everyday after work to relax and on Saturday when you’re fishing and on Sunday while you’re watching the game? Have you ever stopped to think how much money you waste each year on beer? At $4.25 a 6-pack X 365 days a year, that's $1,550!

You might be less stressed if you stopped throwing your money away on booze and started putting it toward your debt.

Chances are, your mama raised you to go to church, but as you got older, you quit going. Perhaps a little "church" would help you out right now.

I must admit that I got away from church during my hell-raising years, but praise God I got my life right with Jesus in 1989. Had I not done so, I would have never been able to cope with the financial disaster that hit my life in 1990.

I WOULD STRONGLY SUGGEST THAT YOU EXCHANGE STRONG DRINK FOR A STRONG RELIANCE AND EVERLASTING FRIENDSHIP WITH JESUS CHRIST.

You might still say, "Hey, it's my business if I drink!" Well, if you've ever lost a day's work because you were too hung over to go to work then it's not just your business is it? It's your employer's business and your family's business because you have taken money from both of them.

Your employer employs you so he can make a profit off your labor. If you don't show up for work, you have cost your boss money and you've lost money.

If you earn $100 a day and you miss one day's work because of a hangover, that's $100 your family doesn't have that month to buy groceries or clothes, or pay utilities or doctor bills. It's $100 they would have had, if you had not spent $10 for a bottle of whiskey that is good for only one thing and that's to MESS UP YOUR LIFE.

DRUGS

If you're into drugs, it's not too late for you to achieve financial freedom. As long as you're still breathing, there is hope.

I got on drugs one time and as innocent as I thought they were, they almost screwed me up. Praise God, I woke up to the fact that they were dulling my senses to a point where I couldn't think, so I stopped "doin' drugs." HOW CAN YOU OR I SUCCEED IF WE CAN'T THINK CLEARLY?

I'm not going to give some long dissertation as to what effects prolonged drug use will have on the human mind and body. I will say this though, some of my friends were as sharp as a tack when we were in high school together, but they decided to experiment with drugs and hallucinatory products in college. Today, they live wasted lives in this great country where opportunities for success are available to everyone.

Oh, my brother or sister, if you're caught up in the drug scene, I encourage you to find help before you waste away. Contact Home of Grace (homeofgrace.org) in Vancleave, MS or Mission at the Cross (missionatthecross.com) in Laurel, MS. They can help.

CIGARETTES

We discussed cigarettes earlier and found that a pack a day costs you $120 a month. And, like I said, this would pay your electric bill, buy fuel for your car for a month, or pay your phone bill. Quitting smoking will also help you live a little longer by saving your lungs.

SPORTS/RECREATION

If you hunt for fun, sell your guns and other huntin' stuff and pay down debt.

If you fish for fun, sell your rod and reel and pay down debt. However, if you fish or hunt to eat, keep on fishing and hunting. If you go boating, sell the boat. If you have a motorcycle that is not your main mode of transportation, sell it. Sell anything that costs you money and is not a necessity in your life, then use that money to pay down debt!

SUCCESS ONLY COMES TO THOSE WHO EXERCISE **SELF-DISCIPLINE** IN EVERY AREA OF THEIR LIVES.

FOOD/DINING

My wife and I took some friends of ours, Darrell and Denise, to dinner at Chuckwagon Buffet one night and spent $45 for our four meals. Shortly thereafter, Darrell and Denise took us to dinner at a fast food restaurant and spent $15 for our four meals.

We have a choice in all things, don't we? What matters is that we make the right decision. Right? Right!

We could afford to take Darrell and Denise to Chuckwagon Buffet. Darrell and Denise could have afforded to take us to Chuckwagon too, but it would have strained their budget.

The four of us had equally good times at both places and I learned a valuable lesson. Both meals filled us up and met the desires of our hunger. But, by going to a fast food joint like Taco Bell, McDonalds or Burger King and paying $15 instead of $45, we could eat there two more times for free! Fast food, especially Taco Bell, is clearly the right choice for those who are earnestly striving for financial freedom.

There is the way of our desires and there is the way of our necessities. If you'll look around, you'll find there are dozens of ways to cut your expenses. Some expense cuts may be bigger than others, and a cost reduction in one area may lead to a cost reduction in another.

Bad habits cost money. SELF-DISCIPLINE will help you break bad habits.

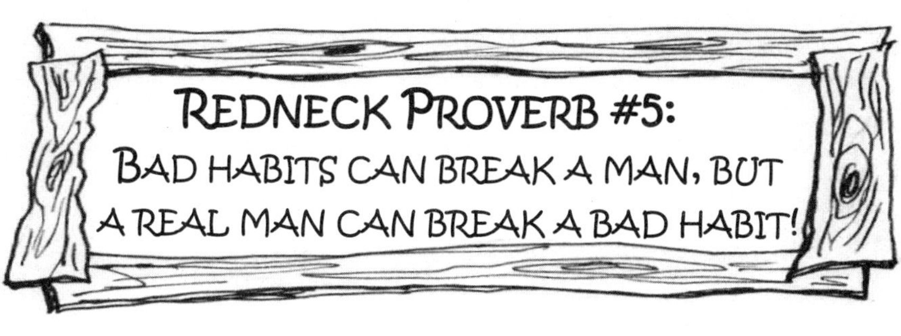

CHAPTER 6

It Ain't Gonna Happen

So you think you can beat the system, huh? I guess you think you're smarter than the person who designed the slot machine, the games of roulette, black jack, poker, dice and countless other games of chance. If so, why are casinos housed in palaces of lavish splendor, while you drive a junker and live in a mobile home? The truth is, the casinos always win.

I once heard about a famous Las Vegas casino owner who had a fleet of Mercedes limousines with bumper stickers that read, "If you don't own a casino, you ought to get one." That one statement alone should tell all of us who the real winners are.

So, where do the casinos get all the money necessary to spend hundreds of millions of dollars on their facilities? From folks like YOU, baby, folks like you!

AIN'T NO SUCH THING AS A WINNER, 'LESSEN THERE'S A LOSER!

Everybody is looking for their pot of gold at the end of some magical rainbow, and even though there are no pots of gold, many folks still think there are. Why? Because we all want something for nothing, however, very few ever succeed in getting anything for free. The "smart cookies" figured out centuries ago that most people are stupid and if they could come up with a big enough prize, most people would do almost anything to get it.

Today, their secret is still the same: simply to convince the gullible that, for a few bucks, they can find the Utopian dream of financial freedom by wagering their hard-earned dollars. Some are lucky, but for the most part only a few ever strike it rich.

If gambling is really beneficial to the gambler, then why are there so many pawnshops in Las Vegas, Reno, Atlantic City and Biloxi? Why do so many people enter the casinos smiling from ear to ear, but leave looking like they've lost their best friend?

I don't know how it is in your state, but the lottery is big in our neighboring state of Louisiana. Millions of lottery tickets are sold monthly for $.50 to $10 each. Yet each week, billboards across the state proudly display an ever-growing lottery jackpot. Where does all the money come from that increases the jackpot? From **YOU**, sucker! Why? Because you lost and will keep on losing as you continue to fall for the pie-in-the-sky tactics of the gambling industry. Remember, it's *your* money that builds the empires of the gaming magnates.

To sum it up best, I'll borrow a phrase (*almost* verbatim) from a song sung by Jerry Reed, "They get the goldmine, you get the shaft!"

I know you're going to do exactly what you want to do regardless of what I say, but my advice to you is this, SAVE YOUR MONEY! Open an interest bearing savings account and put a little away each week. Then, when you're old and gray you'll have enough money for that rainy day, which will surely come!

8:AM (the next morning)

REDNECK PROVERB #6:
NOTHIN' BRINGS SUCCESS BETTER THAN OLD-FASHIONED HARD WORK!

CHAPTER 7

Build Yer Barn First

A few years after World War II ended, the economy of our country was really doing great and new businesses were popping up everywhere. Many of these new businesses wanted to have neon tubing placed around the perimeter of their buildings.

My dad, who was in the sign business, wanted to purchase a neon-making machine for $400. At the same time, my mom wanted a new kitchen, which cost $400. Now, when my mama wanted something she usually got it, but this time Daddy told her, "Daisy, I've got $400 and I can build you a kitchen with it, but if I do I'll never be able to buy the neon machine. However, if you'll let me buy the neon machine first, then I can make another $400 and build your new kitchen."

Mama consented and by year's end Daddy had a fully operational neon shop and Mama had herself a brand new sparkling kitchen. If Mama had been too hardheaded, a new kitchen is all we would have ever gotten with that $400. But, because Daddy got the neon shop first, Mama was able to get a new kitchen too. We prospered wonderfully for many years with the money earned from the neon shop.

The point I'm trying to make here is this: spend your hard-earned dollars on "tools of your trade" rather than on life's pleasures.

You, as a husband, single parent or bachelor, may enjoy working with wood. You may be gifted as a housepainter. You may be a jackleg electrician. You may be a good handyman, a jack-of-all-trades.

You, as a wife, single parent, or single gal, may be gifted as a seamstress. You may have computer skills. You may have a great telephone voice. You may like to write, paint or draw. Your talent may be housekeeping.

Whatever your talent is, put it to good use and make some money with it! If you're not sure what your talent is, think about what you enjoy doing. What are you good at?

THE REWARDS OF *EARLY SELF-SACRIFICE* WILL PAY BIG DIVIDENDS TOWARDS LIFE'S PLEASURES LATER ON.

You and your friends may sit around from time to time and sing together. Well, put those talents to use - **form a singing group!**

If you like to clean - **start a house cleaning service!** Or put that nice voice to work as a **telemarketer!** Who knows, someone may be willing to pay big bucks for your short stories or articles so - **start publishing!** Others may find value in your artwork, so – **start drawing**!

If you enjoy woodworking, get busy **building things!** If you can do just about anything, then go door-to-door **finding odd jobs!**

> "Opportunities are usually disguised as hard work, so most people don't recognize them."
> – Ann Landers

If you're mechanically inclined, sell your TV, disconnect the cable, buy some tools and **start mechanicing** when you get home from your 8 to 5 job.

If you have no skills or talents to speak of and know absolutely nothing about mechanicing, but would like to… **learn!** Go to Amazon.com and buy the book called *Auto Repair for Dummies*. But don't buy a new one that costs a lot of money. Buy a used one for $3.99. You can't get a cheaper education than that.

Pretty soon, you'll be able to quit your job and be a mechanic full time. Then, before you know it, you'll be able to buy another TV with the profits from your mechanic shop. After you've gotten a taste of what you can achieve when you really apply yourself, you won't want to waste time in front of a television again. ('cause you'll be driving a new pickup ...cruising!)

If you have a talent to be a housepainter, quit your low paying job. Get rid of your car, buy a truck, a ladder and some brushes, and **get to painting** houses, commercial buildings, etc.

If your husband works, or if he doesn't, and you can sew, then sell the TV, buy a sewing machine and **start sewing**. Pretty soon, that old couch potato husband of yours will have a bigger and better TV, thanks to you!

Whatever it is you like to do, or are good at, do it!

You will only make a "get by" living working for someone else; real financial freedom comes from working for yourself.

YOU'VE GOT TO TAKE A CHANCE
IF YOU WANT FINANCIAL FREEDOM

A friend of mine told me long, long ago "Build your barn first, Headrick, then you can build your house." I did and now I have both.

The barn in this statement signifies a business. Build your business first then you can enjoy the rewards of your labor.

THAT'S GOOD ADVICE ISN'T IT?

REDNECK PROVERB #7:

IF'N A FELLER HAS THE "WANT TO," GOD'LL HELP HIM WITH THE "KNOW HOW"!

CHAPTER 8

Don't Buy on Impulse!

What does *impulse* mean? It means: I want it and I want it **right now!**

If you've got a million dollars in the bank, you can pick out the car you want, walk in the showroom and write a check for it.

For most folks, however, when they see the car they want, they go in and ask how much down payment money they'll need and how much the monthly payments will be. Then they start figuring out how they can make the deal work. They remember that their tax refund will be here in one month. They could use it to make the down payment and they could work three extra overtime hours each week to earn enough to make the payments. That's all the reasoning some folks do before they say, "I'll take it!"

SELF-DISCIPLINE doesn't even show up for this meeting in their mind. No, sir, some folks make snap decisions for SELF-GRATIFICATION.

After the purchase, however, reality sets in. Oh me, oh my, oh Nehemiah, what am I gonna do?

Oh rats, I didn't know the license plate would cost $500! I didn't think the insurance would cost $50 a month more than I'm paying now! I didn't know it was a gas-guzzler and was going to burn twice the gas my old car did!

Take time to think *before* you buy and you will keep yourself out of a lot of financial trouble.

Don't buy on impulse! **Don't buy on impulse!** I repeat, **DON'T BUY ON IMPULSE**!

CHAPTER 9

Don't Spend Yer Raises

Well, well, well, you got a raise! Congratulations! Are you gonna take that money and pay it on existing debt? No, siree, Bud! You're gonna go out and buy something with it. Right? Sure you are, we all do. Our reasoning is "Hey, my raise is $50 a month, now we can buy that new big screen TV we've been wanting. It only costs $49 a month, **let's buy it!**"

Problem is, your $50 raise is taxable. Forgot about that, huh? So now you're only going to take home $35. However, you've increased your spending $49 per month by buying that new big screen TV. That means you're short $14 per month. See what impulse buying does?

If you would have taken your $50 raise ($35 take home) and paid on existing debt, you would have bettered your financial condition instead of worsening it.

Discipline yourself not to spend your raises or any other unexpected income such as a bonus, tip, commission, or cash from the sale of some miscellaneous item like an old lawnmower or car part.

The whole secret to financial freedom is:

SELF-DISCIPLINE!

SELF-DISCIPLINE!

SELF-DISCIPLINE!

CHAPTER 10

How to Build Yerself A Nest Egg

What is a "nest egg"? Good question!

A nest egg is a stash of cash that smart people set aside for a rainy day - their children's education, a new home, a new car, emergencies or special needs that "pop up" unexpectedly.

However, real smart people put a little cash away each week and forget about it. This money should be untouchable. If it's easily accessible and you lack the SELF-DISCIPLINE to leave it alone, then don't bother. Just spend it all and stay in the mess you're in.

But, if you'll use SELF-DISCIPLINE and stash a little away in a safe place, you'll wake up one morning after you've retired and give yourself a big ol' hug. Your wife will probably give you a face full of sugar, too!

The following simple rules will help you begin to build your own nest egg:

DON'T SPEND ON UNNECESSARY THINGS

Do you really *need* that red whirly-gig thing advertised on TV that relieves stress for $19.95? Of course not! So, put that $19.95 in the bank or pay down debt with it and start to relieve your burden of stress caused by previous acts of sheer stupidity.

> SELF-DISCIPLINE REDUCES STUPID ACTS OF SELF-INDULGENCE

DON'T SPEND FOOLISHLY

What a beautiful coat! Regularly priced at $99.95 it's now on sale for $49.95. Sounds like a good deal, but THINK BEFORE YOU BUY! Put your mind in gear. Remember, you have a perfectly good coat in the closet. So, put that $49.95 in the bank and enjoy the warmth of knowing you have a few bucks in your nest egg. Or use the $49.95 to pay down debt. Remember, you can't wear two coats at once.

You may think this rule doesn't pertain to you because you rarely splurge on big-ticket items; therefore, you think you don't spend money foolishly. Well, what about that fancy, five-dollar-a-cup coffee you drink on a regular basis, just because it's the popular thing to do? Now, that's pretty doggone foolish, if you ask me.

DON'T BUY STUFF JUST BECAUSE YOU WANT IT

Before you purchase a new car or truck, consider this scenario:

Isn't that a pretty car? Isn't it the most beautiful car you've ever seen? The price tag says $500 down and only $200 per month. Your car is worth the down payment and you can swing the $200 monthly payment, "somehow." So, you said you'd take it, didn't you?

Here you go buying on impulse again. If you had put your mind in gear for just a minute, you would have realized these important facts:

A. Your old car was running good, wasn't it?

B. It was getting you around just fine, wasn't it?

C. It was paid for, wasn't it?

D. You had no car note, did you?

E. I bet the license plate was cheaper on your old car, wasn't it?

F. How about insurance? Cheaper on the old one, right? Right!

I know you *want* a new car and you may even *need* a new car, but wait a little longer. Take the $500 down payment and the $200 per month that you would have paid on your new car and put it in the bank for, let's say, one year. In one year, you'll have some extra cash to increase your down payment, which in turn will reduce your monthly payments, which in turn will pay for your new license plate and the insurance costs associated with your new purchase. That's a good reward for one act of SELF-DISCIPLINE.

DON'T BUY WITH CREDIT CARDS

If your goal in life is to be "one up" on your next-door neighbor then read no further and throw this little book in the garbage can. But, if your goal is to achieve financial freedom and accumulate some wealth, then read on.

Mail order catalogs are nice and convenient, but the products they offer are very, very expensive. Catalog companies survive off folks who have one or twenty credit cards. It is so easy to say, "Charge it!" isn't it? Well, saying, "Charge it!" isn't helping build a nest egg for you; it's building a nest egg for the folks who own the company you're buying from. So, throw those catalogs away and cut up your credit cards!

The slogan "Say No to Drugs" may need to be rewritten to read "Say No to Credit Card Spending!" It takes SELF-DISCIPLINE, but YOU CAN DO IT, if you'll just make up your mind to do so.

SOME FOLKS BUY STUFF THEY DON'T NEED TO IMPRESS PEOPLE THEY DON'T EVEN KNOW!

Did you know that it costs more to purchase things with a credit card than it does with a check or cash? Credit card companies survive off folks who use those glistening pieces of plastic. A fee ranging from 2% to 4% is always added to each purchase. If you pay with a credit card, you'll never see this fee, but it's there nonetheless.

I could give you all kinds of examples of how much it actually costs to pay for stuff with credit cards, but you already know that so there's no sense beating a dead horse, is it? I will, however, tell you two horror stories of what happens when you buy too much on credit.

Junior and Betty Sue were in debt! Why? Because they had too many credit cards. For folks without SELF-DISCIPLINE, even *one* is too many!

IF YOU CAN'T PAY CASH FOR IT, WHAT MAKES YOU THINK YOU CAN AFFORD IT WITH 21% INTEREST?

Junior and Betty Sue owed $25,000 to credit card companies and the sad thing is they had nothing to show for it. They had purchased mostly disposable items with their seemingly unlimited credit. The only problem with debt is that one day it will have to be paid back. And so came that day for Junior and Betty Sue.

Were they delinquent? On some cards they were, but for the most part they were current; however, they were only paying the minimum amount required.

If you read the fine print on your credit card contract, you'll find out that sometimes the minimum required payment is less than the interest you owe. If this is the case with your credit cards, your debt will <u>never</u> go down! That's right, it will <u>never</u> go down. As a matter of fact, your debt will actually increase. Why? Because the unpaid interest will be added each month to the unpaid balance and will compound. Compounding means you have to pay interest on interest.

I bought a yacht back in the days when I was squandering my wealth. I told the boat dealer that I would buy the nicest yacht he had if the payments weren't over X dollars per month. He met my demands and I got my yacht!

It wasn't long, however, before I realized I didn't *need* a yacht and that, in my haste to get what I *wanted,* I had failed to count the costs of how much money it would really take to operate it. I threw SELF-DISCIPLINE out the window and bought something I didn't need to satisfy my addiction for "stuff."

I called the dealer and told him to sell my yacht. He immediately got a buyer and sold my yacht for the same thing I paid for it! I was a happy camper until I received the paperwork for the sale of the yacht.

Yes, he sold my yacht for the same amount I paid for it, but because I had needed low payments, a long amortization was required which meant I had been paying less each month than the interest. That meant the unpaid interest was being added to the unpaid principle balance. In other words, I could have paid payments for 20 years and still owed more money than I borrowed.

Most credit cards are set up the same way. When you pay the minimum payment, all you're doing is digging yourself a grave that you'll never get out of.

Stop spending and pay more than the minimum payment. **You must pay full interest and some on principle if you ever want to get out of debt.**

Make purchases with cash or check if possible. Never pay with credit cards and never, never, never finance anything unless it is absolutely necessary.

Commonsense tells us that very limited use of credit cards and frequent use of SELF-DISCIPLINE will increase your nest egg daily.

DON'T BUY THE MOST EXPENSIVE THINGS

There's an identity crisis in America today! If clothes, shoes and accessories don't have the proper symbol or trademark emblazoned somewhere on them, some folks think they can't wear them.

Every few years the word “cool” is redefined according to the latest, greatest designer label. People have spent hard-earned money on everything from a “swoosh” on their shoes to an alligator on their shirt. Some kids (and adults) think if it's not Tommy Hilfiger, Abercrombie & Fitch, Guess, Calvin Klein or Gucci, they’re not wearing it. And for the fashionably insane, of course there's Armani and Versace. If this is you, you definitely need to read this book...over and over and over.

I've never been one to wear name brand clothes. I wear what I like, I don't care who made it. Symbolism is for the rich or those who think they are. Regular folks like us need to use SELF-DISCIPLINE and if the shirt, regardless of who made it, fits...wear it.

DON'T BUY THE LEAST EXPENSIVE THINGS

On the other hand, there are times when spending a few more bucks is better. If your younger children need shoes, consider buying them cheap shoes because they will grow out of them before they ever wear them out. But, if you need a pair of work boots, invest in a good pair that will last a long time and feel good to your feet.

If you need a sofa, use commonsense before you buy. If you still have kids at home, buy an inexpensive sofa because they will ruin it before it wears out. If your kids are grown, invest in a quality sofa that will give you many years of enjoyment.

LIVE MODERATELY, NOT LAVISHLY

Most of us live above our means, don't we? We *want* more of everything than what we *need.* We struggle to obtain things we *think* we must have, but don't need.

We miss life and the true beauty of it by always trying to get more "stuff."

One of the hardest things any of us will ever do is to live within our means. We Americans are not made that way. We were raised to "get more stuff."

My sister, on the other hand, was one of the happiest people I've ever known and she didn't have a "pot to pee in" when compared to the wealthy of our society. But, she was happy.

Her husband was a jerk and she finally left him after raising six real neat kids. When the last one left home so did she. She moved back into our old home place. It needed some work and together we fixed it up like it was when we lived there many, many years ago.

She was content. She went to the store once a week and selected what she NEEDED. She didn't buy groceries on impulse. She planned and even took coupons to get the discounts.

She lived by herself and didn't need much. She drove a compact car that was a 1984 model, and she didn't trade it in on a new one until 1997. She got thirteen years use out of it. We should take note of that.

She only bought clothes when she *needed* them. Yes, she window-shopped and there were things I would hear her say she liked, but she didn't think she had to buy them just because she liked them.

Janet had a decent income and could have lived higher than she did, but she didn't because she had *disciplined* herself to live modestly and enjoy life rather than live lavishly and be burdened down with loads of debt.

Every American, whether rich or poor, could have learned a lot about SELF-DISCIPLINE and the joy of life itself from my sister. She was a wonderful, wonderful lady!

REDNECK PROVERB #10:

YOU BUILD A NEST EGG BY NOT SPENDIN' EVERYTHING YOU ERN!

CHAPTER 11

Become a Knee-go-she-a-ter

Negotiate every price. I repeat, **negotiate every price**. I'm going to say it one more time, **NEGOTIATE EVERY PRICE!**

The printer of this book did not make as much money as he would have made because I negotiated. I didn't negotiate so hard that he wouldn't make a profit, but I did negotiate a good deal for me. And it turned out to be a decent deal for him.

The cost to print this batch of books was $5,000. He was asking $5,365. All I did was ask him to round it off to an even number. After a few minutes of haggling, he said, OK! This few minutes (probably no more than five) made me $365 and that's not bad for a total of 5 minutes work.

That $365 savings, if put into a bank account, would earn 5%, or about $20, per year and that $20 would keep compounding year after year after year. Nest eggs will work for you even while you're sleeping.

One of my favorite negotiating opportunities is motels. I try not to stay in a hotel if the room is over $50 per night when we're traveling by car. If we're on our motorcycle, we won't pay $50, we strive to only pay $25.

Many clean, reputable chain hotels' room rates are only $45-$65 per night. If I'm quoted $65, I ask for $50. If I'm quoted $60, I ask for $50. If I'm quoted $55, I ask for $50. If I'm told $55 is their lowest price, I tell the attendant thanks for doing the best he could, then I leave and try the hotel next door.

No matter where you are, no matter what you're buying, ask for a discount. You may not get one every time but I promise you'll get more discounts than you do rejections.

Back to motels. If I can get a $60 room for $50, then every sixth night is free. Every little bit matters. You could take each night's savings of $10 and put it in the bank for use later or you could pay down on your existing debt – *now!*

You might be wondering why a millionaire would want to stay in a $50 a night motel room when he could afford to stay in a $100 a night room. Realizing that all motel rooms look the same after the lights are out is part of the reason why I've got a million bucks!

DON'T GIVE UP! Earlier on in this book, we talked about negotiating with your creditors to get them to take seventy-five cents, fifty cents, or even twenty-five cents on the dollar. If you succeed, you'll be saving 25%, 50%, or 75% of what you owe.

It won't take long, if you'll be persistent, to save enough for your "nest egg" to look like an overflowing Easter basket of financial prosperity!

But…you must discipline yourself not to spend your savings. In my opinion, you should take this "free money" and use it to pay down debt or put it in the bank. It's your choice, but getting rid of your debt should be your first priority.

CHAPTER 12

Be the Bestest Bargain Hunter

We love Hudson Salvage Centers. Everyday there are good deals at Hudson's, but sometimes they have *special* bargain days!

Typically, Hudson's discounts their items by 25% off the original price. After a while, they lower prices by 40% off the original price, then by 50%, then by 60%, then by 70%, and so on.

One day they had a rack of clothes for sale for 99% off! This meant that each item on this rack would cost 1% of the original price. **One cent on the dollar!** I bought my wife a cashmere skirt that day that originally sold for $100, for $1.

This is what I'm talking about when I tell you to become a bargain hunter.

25% off original price is a pretty good deal.

50% off original price is a better deal.

75% off original price, now that's a good deal, but...

99% off original price, that's a bargain!

You have to shop regularly at Hudson's to get the super spectacular bargains. But, the time invested will be worth it.

My mother-in-law went to Hudson's one Saturday and they had a pile of huge empty bags beside several racks and tables of clothes. You could purchase an empty bag for

$1 and fill it as full of clothes as you could for free. She put two men's leather jackets in one bag and several pairs of ladies pants, jeans, and blouses in the other bag and handed the attendant $2.

When she got home, she unpacked the two bags and found that the original sales prices of the clothes in those two bags totaled $800! Now, THAT'S A BARGAIN!

Bargains are not only at Hudson's, they're everywhere. You just have to look around your city to find them.

DON'T JUST BE A BARGAIN HUNTER,
BE THE **BESTEST** BARGAIN HUNTER
YOU CAN BE!

CHAPTER 13

What's Schoolin' Got To Do With Success?

Most folks say you must have a college education to succeed. Well, I disagree!

I went to summer school for three years and finally graduated high school with a "D" average. My graduating class clapped and cheered when my name was called to receive my diploma. To be honest, I was surprised too!

I knew I wasn't smart enough to go to college, and if I would have, I would have probably failed. So, I went to work with my dad in his sign shop and learned to work with my hands. He taught me to do things correctly and to work hard. I listened, I learned and I WORKED HARD!

For thirty years, I worked six days a week, laboring for 16-18 hours a day. I wanted to succeed and I was willing to pay whatever price it took to be a success.

"THE ONLY PLACE *SUCCESS* COMES BEFORE *WORK* IS IN THE DICTIONARY."
– Vince Lombardi

Like I said, I didn't get a college education, but I did have sense enough to realize that since I wasn't very smart I would have to work twice as hard and twice as long as anyone else if I ever intended to have anything nice.

I did without vacations; I did without the luxury of a nice home; I never did, and still don't, have any hobbies. I do have a Harley-Davidson motorcycle. It took me fifty years to get it, but I finally did. Now each summer my wife, Gina, and I ride it out west on our vacation.

I have never been ashamed for anyone to see me work and get dirty from head to toe. I've never backed away from any type of work either.

We had a septic tank problem at a resort where I was working one time and since I didn't want to ruin my boots, I took them off and jumped in barefooted. We got the job done, but

a few days later my feet and legs began to feel funny. Worms had bored through my skin and were crawling around under my skin. I could see evidence of their movement each morning when I awoke.

It took weeks to rid my body of these worms. And the poison I had to take to kill them made me stink like a bad case of body odor.

Yep, I endured things most people wouldn't endure and I kept on doing work that nobody else wanted to do, but it paid off.

Education is nice and God bless those who have it, but **you *can* be a success without it,** if you'll remember what my daddy said, "YOU CAN HAVE ANYTHING YOU WANT **IF**...YOU'RE WILLING TO WORK HARD ENOUGH, WAIT LONG ENOUGH AND ARE WILLING TO PAY THE PRICE."

If you have the opportunity to get an education, get it. Education is one thing that nobody can ever take away from you. But, **don't ever let anyone tell you that you can't succeed without an education**, because I know better.

I was voted "Most Likely to Fail in Business" during my senior year in High School, but I haven't. I almost did in 1990, but with SELF-DISCIPLINE and HARD WORK, I've not only survived, I've made millions. And just so you know, my wife and I were able to purchase the resort, on the Caribbean island, where I got the worms in my feet.

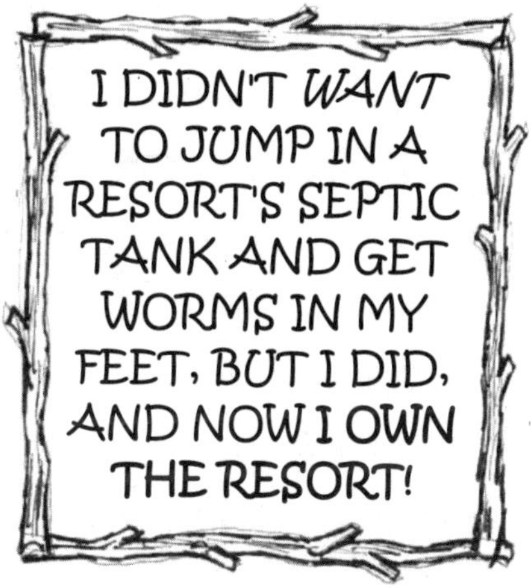

Gina and I have never been accepted into the circles of the Who's Who in our town. Nor are we ever invited to any parties for the affluent, but you know what? It really doesn't matter 'cause we've got our nest egg.

I mentioned earlier that it took fifty years for me to get a Harley. We now have seven, not including our three-wheel “War Wagon.” In addition to the resort where I got the worms in my feet, we own two others and a 7,700 square foot home on 6 acres of land. We have an import/export business in Thailand, 9 sign company sales offices in 6 states, and a plane to get us there. We own two sign manufacturing plants, one in Mississippi and one in North Carolina, and have right at 150 employees on our payroll. Check us out at headricks.com and hellfighters.org to see for yourself what SELF-DISCIPLINE and SERVING JESUS have done for us, and can do for you.

I don't have to work as hard as I did for 30 years anymore. I have a wife who loves me and her love alone makes me a success. Money just makes true love much more fun.

Friend, my desire right now is to help you get your finances in order so you can have everything you want in life, too.

REDNECK PROVERB #13:

A REAL SMART FELLER KNOWS THE VALUE OF A DOLLAR AND A DAY, AND WASTES NEITHER!

CHAPTER 14

What About Yer Young 'uns?

We've talked about financial success and how to achieve it. However, I didn't mention stocks, bonds, mutual funds, investments, securities, and all those things that go along with financial success. They will come later. Right now, all we want to do is get you out of debt as soon as possible so you can put a little nest egg away for a rainy day.

In addition to financial success, there's another arena for success that is just as important, if not more so, and that's your family.

If you're married and have kids, your whole emphasis should be placed on their well-being. All of your personal and financial planning should be with their present and future well-being in mind.

Whatever you accomplish financially will directly affect your children's future.

Some parents however, don't care about the future needs of their children and do only those things that satisfy their personal hunger for self-gratification. I hope this is not the case with you and your children, but facts are facts and whether we like it or not, there are some pretty cold-hearted moms and dads in this world who think only of themselves. If you are one of them, shame on you.

Hopefully, you are one of those who does love your children and wants to see them prosper.

In order for them to prosper however, you must instill into them the principles of fair play, honesty, integrity, trustworthiness, loyalty and hard work.

If you can succeed in planting these character traits in your children, how much or how little money you may accumulate really won't matter, YOUR CHILDREN WILL SUCCEED.

REDNECK PROVERB #14:

FAMILY FIRST, STUFF LAST!

CHAPTER 15

Last Chapter

Uh oh, here it comes. Yep, something's gotta be said about my Lord and Savior, Jesus Christ.

You may be just like I was many years ago when every mention of Jesus Christ by some folks turned me off. If what I'm about to say turns you off, I hope you'll still hang in here with me for just two or three more minutes. What I want to tell you is true and may change your life, as it did mine.

Hopefully, this book has helped you take a long, hard look at your financial situation. If you've discovered that you may be headed in the wrong direction financially, start now to better your financial position. **But, don't expect to get out of the mess you're in overnight!** Be patient and use the practical applications in this book, then good things will begin to happen!

As I've said earlier, I almost went broke in 1990 and if an experience had not occurred in my life in 1989, I would probably be reading someone else's book on financial freedom instead of writing one.

Let me tell you a little story about the Rhino Man. Yep, that's me, Richard the Rhino Man.

> My life has been one of excitement and adventure. I've climbed the Andes Mountains in Peru, canoed on the Amazon, and instead of the piranha eating me, I've eaten them. I've searched for gold in the jungles of Central America and pursued men who had it. I've survived terrorist

attacks in South America and Central America, walked away from three airplane crashes, been shot at, beat up, cut with a knife and had my head fractured with a blow from a pistol. I've even been locked up in a Honduran jail for robbing ancient Mayan ruins.

I was having the time of my life, but deep down inside I was miserable. So miserable, in fact, that one day while piloting my twin-engine airplane, I pointed it downward and dove toward the ground at over 200 mph, intending to end my life. But, seconds before impact, God spoke to me and said, "Pull up boy, 'cause I'm not finished with you yet." I missed death and hell by seconds, and thanks to a loving and miracle-working God, you can too.

I lived a double life during and after my first marriage, doing things I never thought I was capable of. But one day a man came to see me and told me that outwardly I appeared happy, but he knew that deep down I was truly miserable. He began to tell me about Jesus Christ and how Jesus died for me. He said that if I would turn my life over to Jesus and submit myself to Him and adhere to the teachings of God's Word, then I would find true happiness.

I had heard this pitch about Jesus many times before, but this time I felt like I really needed true peace in my life. I was over-indulging in drugs, sex, and everything else that was not good for me. I abused them all in excess. But in February 1989, I gave up on trying to do life alone! I gave in to Jesus Christ and WOW! what a difference He has made in my life.

Today, I am happily married to a wonderful, Christian lady. We are financially secure; we own our own home and several nice vehicles. Our business is booming, our love for our

> Savior is consuming, and the happiness that has followed my commitment to Jesus Christ has been unbelievable.
>
> I don't know if you're hurting inside like I was and to the point where life no longer holds the glamour it once did for you, but if you are, there is HOPE! His name is JESUS!

The story you've just read is true. I know it's true because it's my story. You can take it or leave it, but if you'll believe what I've told you and trust in Jesus, He will save you and fill your life with the same abundant joy and peace that I have.

If you don't believe me, get a copy of the Bible and read Romans 6:23 which says, *For the wages of sin is death; but the gift of God is eternal life through Jesus Christ our Lord.* Then read John 3:16, which says, *For God so loved the world that He gave His only begotten son, that whosoever believeth in Him should not perish but have everlasting life.* Romans 10:9 says, *That if thou shalt confess with thy mouth the Lord Jesus, and shalt believe in thine heart that God hath raised Him from the dead, thou shalt be saved.*

Salvation is free! All you have to do is ask Jesus to save you.

I almost died in my sins, but praise God, He extended to me His forgiving grace and He will extend the same forgiving grace and mercy to you if you will just ask Him to.

If you want peace, happiness and joy in your life then please bow your head and pray this prayer:

> *Jesus, I know if I died right now I'd go to hell. Please forgive me of my sins, save me, and fill my life with the peace, happiness and abundant joy that Richard the Rhino Man said You have for me. Amen.*

Friend, salvation is sometimes difficult at first because old habits may still dominate your life. Find yourself some Christian friends and let them help you get started on your walk through the peaceful valley of joy and happiness toward our eternal home in Heaven where you and I will live and reign with Jesus forever and ever.

If you're where I was, fed up, beat down and from the surface it looks like there is nowhere to turn, then turn it all over to Jesus. He's a forever friend and will give you the strength and courage you need to face each new day head on regardless of the obstacles and hardships the day may hold.

By receiving Jesus Christ as your Savior and letting Him become Lord of your life, you will also receive the power and permission to talk directly with the sovereign God who created all things. Through His Son's name you can ask Him for help. It makes no difference what your needs are, nothing is too difficult for our Holy and all-powerful Heavenly Father to handle.

I'm here to tell you, brother or sister, that I care about you and your finances. I care about your family. I care about your eternity. And if I care about you, who I probably don't even know, just imagine how much more our Heavenly Father cares about you.

The Bible says in Matthew 10:29-31 that not a single sparrow will fall to the ground without His noticing it. If something as small and insignificant as a sparrow, having a problem, would get God's attention, just imagine the attention you, as one of His children, will get when you have a problem.

Trust Jesus Christ as your Lord and Savior today. I did in 1989 and my life has been so wonderfully different since then I can hardly believe it myself.

Conclusion

It takes more than having lots of money or "stuff" to bring true joy into your life. And I hope this little book has planted some seeds that will bring **spiritual** and **financial freedom** to you and your family.

You deserve a nice home, a nice car, nice clothes and peace in your heart. I want you to get all of them and you can, if you'll let SELF-DISCIPLINE and JESUS CHRIST control your life. Learn to say NO to your impulses and bad habits. It will be hard at first, but it will become easier with time and pretty soon shouts of joy will resound from your lips as you realize that you had the ability to succeed all along, but you never knew how to go about it.

I hope I've helped you a little in your quest to gain financial freedom, but if financial freedom and accumulated wealth elude you, do not despair; if you discover the joy of the Lord while working through your problems, that's all that really matters in life anyway. He'll then be with you through the good times and the bad.

Regardless of what happens from this point on, always remember EGBAR.*

---

* Everything's Gonna Be All Right

Final Thoughts Fer You to Remember

1. Set yer budget and stik to it!
2. Don't buy on impulse!
3. Don't spend yer hard-earned money on dumb stuff!
4. Don't buy stuff with credit cards!
5. Be the bestest bargain hunter you can be!
6. Figure out what yer good at and git after it!
7. Don't be a couch potato; sell the TV and git to work!
8. If somethin' kin be done, and you think you kin do it, then do it!
9. Start yerself a nest egg.
10. Don't obligate yerself fer more than you can afford.
11. Knee-go-she-ate the price of everthang.
12. If you didn't git no schoolin', then you gotta work harder and longer than everbody else!

Remember the things I've just told you! Let them become imbedded in your brain. Exercise them daily; let them guide you toward financial freedom.

TO SUM IT UP...

Financial freedom and accumulated wealth are achieved by doing what you don't want to do when you don't want to do it. Doing what I didn't want to do when I didn't want to do it paid off for me and it will pay off for you, **if**...
you're willing to
work hard enough,
wait long enough,
and are willing
to pay the
price!

ABOUT THE AUTHOR

Richard Headrick is a successful businessman whose passion is writing encouraging and thought provoking books for members of the whole family.

Richard has written many books, including:

The Well

The Circular Rings of Kansas

Poor Richard's Proverbs

The Treasures of Solomon

Goliath's Fall

America's Churches through the Eyes of a Bum

Hellfighters Operations Manual 1: The Call of a Hellfighter

Hellfighters Operations Manual 2: The Commission of a Hellfighter

Hellfighters Operations Manual 3: The Conflict of a Hellfighter

The Enemy of Heaven

The Seven Churches

My Other Little Book on The Seven Churches

Love Letters from a King

God, If We're the Best You've Got, You're in Big Trouble

Why Everybody Needs Jesus

Last Ounce of Courage

Richard has also written Gospel tracts, including:

Richard the Rhino Man

Hellfighters

Have a Great Day!

Orangevestitis

Will Someone Plant a Tree for You?

Something Special

Guardian Angels

Is Hell Right for You?

There's Only One Thing Better Than a Hummer

In the Company of Fish

The War Wagon

Nickel Tissue

The World is Ablaze

Keeping Christ in Christmas

I'm Here for the Party!

SATAN SUCKS

Some books and tracts are out of print, but may still be available through various sources. Go to hellfighters.org or send us an e-mail to info@hellfighters.org to order these books and other items that are available. If we've got it in stock, then you've got it. If we don't have it, we'll tell you who may have it and where you might be able to get it. If nobody has 'em, it means you've waited too late and missed out.

It's OK to miss out on these books, but don't mess around and miss out on Heaven.

Other Hellfighter Productions

Keeping Christ in Christmas – audio CD
Christians Still Die – 15 minute documentary on DVD
Last Ounce of Courage – 2 hour feature film on DVD

HEAVEN'S SWEET, HELL'S HOT, YOU'RE GOING TO ONE, READY OR NOT!

HELLFIGHTER PUBLICATIONS
One Freedom Square, Laurel, MS 39440-3367
601-649-HOPE
hellfighters.org
info@hellfighters.org